CHU
MEDITATION

A STEP-BY-STEP GUIDE

OTHER BOOKS BY C.K.CHU

Tai Chi Chuan Principles and Practice
The Book of Nei Kung

A note on the use of Chinese language in this book:
English transliterations of Chinese characters are based on
Master Chu's native Cantonese dialect

CHU
MEDITATION

A STEP-BY-STEP GUIDE

C. K. CHU

Illustrations by Dan Giella

Sunflower Press

NEW YORK

Published by SUNFLOWER PRESS,
P.O. Box 750733, Forest Hills Station, NY 11375
Distributed by CHU TAI CHI
156 W. 44th Street, NY, NY 10036 • www.chutaichi.com

Chu Meditation; a step-by-step guide.
ISBN: 0-9616586-2-2
Library of Congress Control Number: 2002105443

Illustrations: Dan Giella
Cover photo: Michael Smith
Design: Elizabeth Sharpe

First Edition

ACKNOWLEDGMENTS

*First and foremost, I am fortunate to have had Nathaniel Wice's
assistance in writing, organizing and refining the text.
His intelligence, integrity, and light-hearted seriousness have been invaluable;
this work would not have been possible without him.
My ardent thanks to Dan Giella for his beautifully rendered illustrations,
and to my daughter, Elizabeth, for design & layout.
Thanks also to Cynthia Elmas for her meticulous editing work
and to my wife, Carol, for her help, as always, at each stage of production.
For careful readings and feedback, I am indebted to
Dimitri Ehrlich, Joseph Barbarino, Margaret Divan, Joel Jayson,
Kristan Maher, and Elisabeth Wilds.
For continual support, and generosity,
I am grateful to all of my students and my family.*

For my daughter, Linda

TABLE OF CONTENTS

Introduction

MEDITATION
— WHY?

MEDITATION is an ancient tool, used since recorded time by the major cultures of the world. In China, the philosophies of Buddhism, Confucianism, and Taoism each emphasize meditation as a powerful way to obtain a clear or empty mind. The Chinese words for meditation, "*jing dzwo*" (靜坐) translate literally as "sitting quietly".

The journey to achieving this state of being motionless, with body and mind silent, builds mental strength and flexibility the same way physical exercise helps develop the body. The benefits are straightforward—a clear mind is necessary to restore balance to your life, to reduce stress and to explore your true path, or *tao* (道). Sitting quietly also helps to cultivate the flow of energy (*chi*, 氣). For these reasons, most high-level martial arts practitioners meditate as part of their daily training.

Every person is unique, with his or her own potential to be happy and fulfilled. However this uniqueness is rarely aligned with the world we live in. It can be stifled by economic obligations, family responsibilities, prejudices, or just about any other customs and laws. As a result, we consciously or unconsciously choose to please others rather than ourselves. Society or family, for instance, may pressure you to strive for a prestigious occupation like law or medicine when it may not make you happy.

You may ask: Why don't I see a therapist, or live on my own somewhere away from family and other obligations and pursue my own interests? Well, seeing a therapist is good if the therapist is able to know and carefully guide you. But, of course, the therapist will never know you as well as you know yourself. The fact is that you know yourself best. The important thing is not to suppress your interests, nor just do what everybody else wants you to do. This suppression will actually harm you and, to the extent it frustrates you, may result in harm to others. To live alone may seem like a good solution. But meditation will help you without the need to leave your family, or society in general. Meditation gives you a fresh start. In China, people also talk about leaving society to become a monk. But there is a well-known saying that when you become a monk and join a monastery, you are then going to have monastic problems.

This cultivation of quietness, essential for clear thinking, may be more crucial than ever. Nowadays we are bombarded by a tremendous amount of information. In print, on television, or via the internet, scandals, sound bites, and commercials distract us, influence us. With so much going on, people can easily lose sight of what is important in their lives, and to the welfare of our world. Meditation slows down your train of thought so that you can evaluate all this information and check that you're going in the right direction, instead of just going and going.

It is easy to imagine oneself meditating serenely within the ancient walls of a temple in the Himalayas, but can you picture yourself sitting quietly amid the swirling crowds and flashing neon of New York City's Times Square? I chose the cover of this book because my school is a half-block away, but also because you don't have to be physically present at this crossroads of the world to feel as if your life were also at times a kaleidoscopic blur of light and sounds, of people on parade: protesting, performing, peddling, or preaching.

Today, the key to effective meditation remains the same as it was in ancient times: daily practice. You can start with as little as fifteen minutes a day. Stick with the techniques I have laid out in this book for just a few weeks, and I'm sure you'll find meditation invaluable.

C. K. CHU
Times Square
June, 2002

I.

PREPARATION

Chapter One

THE BENEFITS OF MEDITATION

B ENEFITS. There are many benefits to meditation practice, but the only way to really appreciate the benefits of meditation is through your own experience. Even though each individual's development is different, there are some general benefits to look for, starting with the most immediate.

1.1 CALMING EFFECT
The simple fact that you're making a point of sitting quietly will help you reduce stress. You have a chance to catch your breath. You're able to approach new endeavors with a fresh mind.

1.2 PHYSICAL HEALING
The stretching will strengthen the lower back and legs, making them more flexible and correcting their alignment. A strong lower back and strong legs will help the internal organs, especially the kidneys. The kidneys are the most important organs for vitality, strength, and sexual energy. Kidneys are the key to the body's production of *chi*. Healthy kidneys will keep your body youthful.

1.3 CULTIVATE *CHI*

Meditation works on internal energy—called *chi*—in several ways: through the alignment of the body, the quieting of the mind, and the practice of deep breathing.

Chi is the basis of acupuncture and traditional Chinese medicine, where it is considered the most important factor in health. When the *chi* is weak, the person falls ill; when the body fails to produce *chi*, death results. Alternatively, when you meditate the *chi* life force will nourish every cell in the physical system, from the bone marrow to the skin.

You can read more about *chi* in my *Tai Chi Chuan Principles and Practice* and *The Book of Nei Kung*.

1.4 MENTAL PERSPECTIVE

As the calming effect becomes more profound, your thinking will take on a new clarity and freshness. You'll find you have perspective—you're focused and sharp instead of scattered and disoriented. You discover your own personal nature (*sing*, 性), emerging from deep meditation with an awareness of your true interests in life. This sense of self enables you to make better decisions, differentiating between the important and the trivial.

1.5 ETERNAL SPRING

Meditation leads to enlightenment. At a high-level of practice you can meditate for a long time and reach a new stage of consciousness. When you reach that stage, you will feel as if all secrets are revealed and everything suddenly seems so obvious and clear. There are no obstacles. Taoists talk about this as heaven, earth, and self in harmony — the mind, body and universe as one. There is no internal or external conflict or contradiction.

Taoists have a special name associated with this kind of "true feeling" that comes with the practice of high-level meditation: *Jung Yun* (真人; *Jung* meaning "Real," *Yun* meaning "Person"). The Real Person sees things as they are, not colored by taboos from religion, culture, or the judgments of others. Being a *Jung Yun* means that you are not phony. You are true to yourself and true to your beliefs. In other words, the *Jung Yun* sees the essence of life and acts accordingly. You've got no time to play the games that other people play.

Meditation, more than any other practice I've experienced, has revealed to me the essence of life, which is pursuing your own *tao*, preserving your health, fulfilling your potential and seeking intrinsic happiness. The Cantonese call this ideal state, *but low chun* (不老春)—eternal spring, staying young forever.

Chapter Two

YOUR MEDITATION
ENVIRONMENT

T HE BASIC IDEA OF meditation is to sit quietly for a long
time, however if your body is not comfortable then you won't be able
to sit still.

These instructions may seem elaborate the first time you read them,
especially for a practice that's supposed to simplify life. But in teaching
I've found that this kind of structure can make a big difference for the
beginner.

2.1 WHEN TO PRACTICE

It's best to make the habit of practicing in the morning, but you can also
add more meditation at other times of the day. I don't recommend practicing before going to bed, however, because meditation may energize the
body and make it hard to fall asleep. Also, if you practice during the day,
don't do it on a full stomach—try to leave two hours after a light meal or
three hours after a heavy one. By the same token, it's also difficult to meditate if you are very hungry because you'll be thinking about food. The
same logic applies to other bodily functions.

2.2 WHERE TO PRACTICE

Pick a quiet space where you won't be disturbed for a long period of time—for example, maybe in a bedroom early in the morning. Make sure the room has ventilation, but try to avoid direct drafts. Although it's preferable for the space to be dark, you can also try experimenting with sunglasses to block out light.

2.3 WHAT TO WEAR

Your body will usually heat up from meditation, so I recommend loose clothing, preferably made of cotton, that allows your body to breathe. The main rule with your clothing is that you don't want it to disturb you by constricting circulation or making you too hot or too cold.

2.4 WHERE TO SIT

Sit on a flat surface like a bed or the floor. The surface should be firm and also insulated from any cold with a mat or folded towel. You may also want a pillow or cushion to raise up your seat if your knees pop up when you sit cross-legged on the floor.

Some people have trouble sitting comfortably and have a tendency to roll back. In this case, you can lean your back against a wall or something else solid for support. Use a firm pillow to insulate your back from the additional contact.

If sitting on the floor is especially uncomfortable or impossible for some other reason, the next best thing is to sit with your legs over the edge of a chair or bed. Make sure the feet don't dangle—they should rest flat on the floor.

Chapter Three

WARM-UP
STRETCHING

S T R E T C H I N G is an essential preparation for meditation. Most people don't realize how badly their bodies are misaligned. The relaxation that comes from proper stretching helps correct these problems, in turn enhancing the flow of *chi* for the entire body.

3.1 STRETCHING RIGHT LEG

Take the right foot and pull it up with your hands so it sits as high up as possible on the left thigh. Then gently press down on the right knee with the right palm, turning the right palm slightly inward and the right elbow slightly out. At the same time, hold the right foot in place with the left hand, sit up as straight as possible, and try to relax (fig. 3.1).

You should feel the stretch through the whole leg, connecting the toes to the hip, and the hip to the lower back.

You may feel stiff and find it difficult to keep the right knee down even with the palm pressing on it, but don't push down too hard. It's common to feel strain in the arch or ankle of the foot, and later on in the knee.

Fig. 3.1 Stretching Right Leg

Again, it's okay to be a little uncomfortable but it shouldn't be painful—don't force anything.

Hold this for about three minutes.

3.2 STRETCHING LEFT LEG

Repeat the same stretch on the other side with the left leg. Now you're pulling the left foot over the right thigh (with the right hand), and pressing down gently on the left knee (with the left hand).

You will probably find that the stretch on one side is much easier than on the other. Suppose you find that your left leg is stiffer—it's usually a sign that the left hip is tight and not so well aligned (and vice versa for the right side). This misalignment affects your sitting, standing and other aspects of daily life. It causes people to favor the more flexible side, blocking the circulation of *chi*. In a way this stiffness can be a useful diagnostic—your body is telling you to spend more time stretching the tighter side.

These stretches are included here as preparation for the meditation posture; they are also good even if you're doing other stationary activities such as watching television or reading.

Chapter Four

THE MEDITATION POSTURE

静坐姿勢

THERE ARE several possible combinations of sitting and hand positions, but in each case the most important consideration is your flexibility for the sitting posture. Many beginners are able to do the Half Lotus posture even if it is slightly uncomfortable at first—that's what I explain here along with the Tai Chi Hands position. (If you want to experiment with either a less strenuous posture or more advanced techniques, see "Optional Techniques," pages 55, 58-61.)

4.1 HALF LOTUS SITTING POSTURE

To get into the Half Lotus posture on the right side, take the right foot and pull it up with your hands so it sits as high as possible on the left thigh (fig. 3.1). For an example of this posture with Tai Chi Hands (explained below), see figure 4.1. You can do the Half Lotus on the left side by switching the feet. You should alternate legs every time you sit down to practice. (See pages 55, 58-61 for other sitting postures.) During each session of meditation if you feel uncomfortable, you can switch legs, but don't forget to switch hands as well.

Fig. 4.1 Half Lotus with Tai Chi Hands

4.2 YIN-YANG HANDS (TAI CHI HANDS)

There are several possible hand positions (others are covered in "Optional Techniques") but I've found that Tai Chi Hands is the most efficient because the fingers connect with meridians, creating a kind of *chi* circuitry.

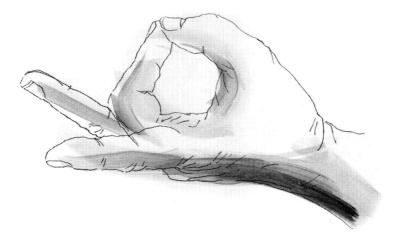

Fig. 4.2a Touch tip of middle finger and thumb of left hand

Fig. 4.2b Lay left hand into palm of right

INSTRUCTIONS:

1. Form a circle by touching the tip of the left hand's middle finger to the tip of the left hand's thumb (fig. 4.2a).

2. Lay the left hand in the open palm of the right hand (fig. 4.2b).

3. Touch the right thumb to the base of the left middle finger (the point on the left hand between the middle finger and the index finger—where the middle finger meets the palm).

Fig. 4.2c Tai Chi Hands creates a yin-yang symbol

From the top, the fingers of the two hands now form a yin-yang symbol (fig. 4.2c). Rest these hands in your lap.

For an example of these hands with Full Lotus, see figure 7.3; for Half Lotus, see figure 4.1.

If you reverse the Half Lotus legs (so that the left foot is being pulled up), then you should also reverse the Tai Chi Hands (so that the right hand is laying in the left). For the "Buddha" and "Crane" hand positions—see pages 60-61.

4.3 BACK STRAIGHT

Straighten and stretch the spine by sitting as tall as possible, as if your head were being pulled from above. This alignment is explained in more detail in "Head Suspended" (page 25).

4.4 EYES HALF-CLOSED

The eyes should be open slightly so you see some light in front of you, but not fully open. Fix the eyes on a particular spot, looking forward and down at an approximate angle of 45 degrees. In the beginning, your eyes may get tired or start to water—this is common and is part of the training.

4.5 EARS NOT HEARING

Try not to listen to any sound. If a sound comes, try to reflect it back by focusing on each of the five steps discussed in the following chapter. If sound is a major problem, I suggest that you experiment in the beginning with earplugs.

4.6 MOUTH CLOSED

Close the mouth, with the teeth touching and the tongue relaxed. The tip of the tongue should rest, touching the front of the top palate where the palate ends at the teeth. Like the Tai Chi Hands, this forms another important meridian connection. The face should be slightly smiling. When the face is smiling it helps relax the entire body. Once the body is relaxed and calm, the mouth will generate extra saliva, indicating that the meditation is having an effect. Swallow the saliva as a kind of nourishment. When you begin to experience the saliva as sweet, that's a sign that your system is working well and that your meditation is becoming more advanced.

4.7 BODY RELAXED

Your whole body should be relaxed, so that your straight back and suspended head help the shoulders drop.

4.8 MENTAL ATTITUDE

For successful meditation, your mental attitude is just as important as the physical alignment. Even if there is something coming right after the meditation that you have been anticipating for a long time—a job interview, a wedding celebration!—you need to keep reminding yourself that this time is for meditation, not for any other agenda. You can also remind yourself that there's no rush, that you have a lot of time, that this time is for rest and recuperation.

II.

MEDITATION

靜坐

五步朱静坐

Chapter Five

THE FIVE STEPS OF CHU MEDITATION

OVERVIEW. You've already done Warm-Up Stretching and chosen a Meditation Posture. Your body is looser from the sitting and stretching— Now you're ready to meditate.

The meditation that I teach consists of five steps. Each step sets the stage for the next, towards the ultimate goal of sitting quietly with a well aligned, balanced body and an empty mind. Although, at first, the steps require some thought, the ultimate goal of meditation is no thought. The five steps are:

1. *Head Suspended*
2. *Deep Breathing*
3. *Mind to the Tan Tien*
4. *Counting 1-10*
5. *Emptying the Mind*

In the following pages, I'll take you through each of these steps individually.

Start with the first step, *Head Suspended*. In the beginning you should spend five minutes on it. This may seem like a short time, but for a beginner even sitting quietly five minutes with the head suspended is a challenge. Once you are comfortable with five minutes, you can gradually increase the time over the months to ten or more minutes. *Head Suspended* should be the only meditation exercise for the first two weeks of your daily practice.

After that, you can start adding steps in order, one at a time every two weeks. This means you'll be working on all five steps at the start of the ninth week (fig. 5.1). Each time you practice, you will go through each of the steps you've worked up to. For instance, in the fifth week you'll be doing five minutes of *Head Suspended*, then five minutes of *Deep Breathing*, then five minutes of *Mind to the Tan Tien*, for a total single session of 15 minutes. The temptation to combine steps in the beginning should be avoided. When it's time to do the second step, for example, forget the first step. You should not be focusing on two things simultaneously.

How do you time the steps? You can use a soft alarm, like a quiet clock radio, to measure the total time. The exact time for the individual steps is not as important as being relaxed and meditative, but you can also measure them separately if it doesn't require too much attention (some wristwatches, for instance, have a countdown timer that can be set to automatically beep every five or ten minutes).

BEGINNING MEDITATION SCHEDULE

WEEK	STEP TO ADD	DAILY MEDITATION TIME
1-2	*Head Suspended*	5 minutes
3-4	*Deep Breathing*	10 minutes
5-6	*Mind to the Tan Tien*	15 minutes
7-8	*Counting*	20 minutes
9-10	*Emptying the Mind*	25 minutes

Fig. 5.1

Step One:

HEAD
SUSPENDED

*H*EAD SUSPENDED is the first of the five steps, and it marks the transition from Warm-Up Stretching to the mindfulness of meditation. The basic idea is to suspend the head and relax, but even this simple step takes practice while offering valuable benefits.

HOW TO DO IT

Sit with your back straight, so that your head and spine are suspended like a string of beads held up from above. Tuck the chin in slightly and imagine the top of your head being pulled straight up. It's as if you're trying to be taller than you are.

Your mind will wander but make an effort to focus any thoughts back to maintaining this uplifted posture, stretching the spine. If you continue to have trouble concentrating, you can repeat to yourself "head suspended, head suspended, head suspended" as a way of drowning out other thoughts.

BENEFITS

Even this simple exercise can alleviate back problems. *Head Suspended* both stretches and strengthens the spine, and can correct years of bad alignment. A strong, flexible back is also important for the circulation of *chi* to the head, to the organs, and to the rest of the body

COMMON PROBLEMS

The two major physical difficulties for beginning meditation students are backache and numbness in the legs.

Backache is an indication of back problems, either major or minor. When you hold the meditation posture, you're realigning your back to the optimal position. This sometimes hurts. Your body reacts and you have pain. But it is a healing pain. As time goes by, the pain will disappear. For some people this takes days, for others months or years.

When your legs fall asleep, it's because the circulation is blocked. This exercise will help you open it up. Use your own judgement about how hard to push—you may want to experiment with shorter periods of meditation interspersed with more frequent stretching. See also "Self-Massage for Legs" on page 49.

Step Two:

DEEP
BREATHING

*T*HE FIRST STEP, *Head Suspended*, helped stretch the body. Done correctly, this relaxes the body and induces more comfortable, healthy breathing. Now we're going to take this relaxed breathing and refine it into one of the basic meditative techniques.

HOW TO DO IT

With the mouth closed, inhale slowly through the nose, pushing the diaphragm down so that the lower abdomen expands and pushes outward. (For the expansion of the abdomen, the lower the better.) Then exhale slowly—also through the nose with the mouth closed—contracting the abdomen to push air out of the lungs. This is sometimes called diaphragm breathing.

There are four key qualities of *Deep Breathing*: long, deep, small, smooth. They're very important and worth memorizing. Each breath should be a small flow of air, drawn deep with the diaphragm, long in duration, and in a smooth, even breathing pattern when both inhaling and exhaling.

When you think of "deep," imagine that you are pushing the inhaled air down below the navel, even to the ground—Chuang Tzu, the Taoist philosopher, actually says to breathe to the soles of the feet.

BENEFITS

Air is the most important nourishment for cultivating *chi*, even more than water or food. *Deep Breathing* literally transforms air (external *chi*) to the life force, internal *chi*. When done correctly, *Deep Breathing* also helps relax the body and accelerate the healing process. It's the basis of the commonsense advice to "relax and take a deep breath."

COMMON PROBLEMS

Beginners have problems breathing down into the diaphragm; it just takes practice. Whether it's for meditation or singing opera, *Deep Breathing* is a technique to learn, not a simple instruction to follow. Focus on the four concepts and you will improve with practice, but do not get discouraged if, in the beginning, your "long" is not so long and your "deep" is not so deep. As you practice, work to make the breath longer, deeper, smaller, and even more regular. Once the body is breathing correctly, it is deep in a meditative state.

After at least half a year of daily training, you can experiment with variations. Sometimes a sound is employed to help extend the duration of the exhale—see "Optional Techniques" (pages 55-57) for more information.

Step Three:

MIND TO
THE TAN TIEN

$\mathcal{H}$AVING PROGRESSED through *Head Suspended* (Step One) and *Deep Breathing* (Step Two), your body should be quite relaxed by this point. *Head Suspended* and *Deep Breathing* should continue automatically. This state of physical alignment prepares you for the more focused mental practice of meditation.

In this transitional step, you want to use your mind to gather the body's energy in its *chi* center, the *tan tien* (see below for further information). You can compare the mind focused on the *tan tien* to a magnifying lens concentrating sunlight into an intense pinpoint. This step, along with the previous *Deep Breathing*, is sometimes called the "Wind-Fire technique" by Taoists—the wind is the breathing and the fire is the *Mind to the Tan Tien*.

HOW TO DO IT
Deep Breathing has already brought your *Mind to the Tan Tien*. All that's required is more focus.

It may sound strange to talk about focusing the mind on a particular part of the body, but it's easy to experience—just try, for instance, closing your right hand into a fist, and then extend and stretch the pinky finger in and out of the fist. Your mind is now "in" the right pinky.

Similarly, you can put your *Mind to the Tan Tien*. The *tan tien* is not a meridian point; it's an area about two inches below the navel, inside the body—right in the center—between the front and the back. (It's interesting that this particular area is also the center of gravity of the whole body.) To feel the *tan tien*, put your thumb in your navel and use your other four fingers to push into yourself, just underneath. Then do *Deep Breathing*. On the inhale you should feel a core hardening inside, like a basketball being inflated. That's your *tan tien*. In the beginning, if necessary, you can press the *tan tien* with your fingers to help focus your mind there.

BENEFITS

Mind to the Tan Tien stores up the body's energy. Up until now we've used mental energy to focus on physical goals like *Head Suspended* or *Deep Breathing*; here we're using mental energy to concentrate *chi* in the body's *chi* reservoir. Once stored and concentrated, *chi* will circulate more vigorously in the whole body, just like a dam that gathers and channels water for irrigating fields. Nourishing both crops and the body, then, require similar techniques.

COMMON PROBLEMS

Mind to the Tan Tien helps you concentrate on your body, which is in and of itself beneficial—when your mind is there, the *chi* will be there. But most people aren't accustomed to directing their thoughts inward. The exterior of the body is obvious and apparent; it's what you can see and touch. The interior, however, is only considered when we have discomfort or pain. So the first difficulty is just turning the mind inward to the body. It takes practice and patience. The pinky exercise, described above, can help both to focus the mind and to visualize the exact location of the *tan tien*.

Another common problem with *Mind to the Tan Tien* is recognizing progress. You should know that you probably won't see dramatic results right away. It can take two or three years of normal daily training before you feel some heat (*chi*) in the *tan tien*. When you do get that feeling, it's considered a real accomplishment. I still remember my first time—it was quite a surprise, and then it became regular.

Step Four:

COUNTING

LET'S ANALYZE what we've been doing so far. First we aligned the body with the sitting posture and *Head Suspended*. This puts the body in a comfortable state so it's ready to sit still for a long time.

Then we started working on the circulation of energy with *Deep Breathing* and focusing the *Mind to the Tan Tien*. These steps are necessary—and extremely beneficial—but they still involve the mind, which we ultimately want to empty.

Counting is the transition to the fifth and final step of *Emptying the Mind*. You can think of the whole process as a rocket launch. *Head Suspended* and *Deep Breathing* are the physical launching pad, *Mind to the Tan Tien* is the ignition. *Counting* is the countdown to blast-off from earth into the empty space and effortless orbit of *Empty Mind*. Each time you meditate, you want to repeat the entire journey, from launching pad to orbit.

HOW TO DO IT

To begin *Counting*, forget about the *tan tien* and start repeating the numbers one to ten at a comfortable pace in your head. It's important that you don't count your breathing—which you coordinate with the breath; then you're still thinking about the breathing, which we want to forget. Also, try not to visualize the numbers for the same reason. Your pace should be continuous and unvarying—so monotonous that it puts the mind at rest.

BENEFITS

With the body already aligned and energized, *Counting* helps the further circulation of *chi* by removing more mental distractions. When the mind disengages from the everyday world, both mind and body have a chance to rest, recharge and recuperate. Many other systems of meditation rely on counting, visualization or a mantra technique—but stop there. We shall go further.

COMMON PROBLEMS

It's very difficult to leave other thoughts behind and focus exclusively on *Counting*. Just like all the other steps, it gets more comfortable as time goes by. If you have trouble concentrating on the numbers, try adapting the same technique I described for *Head Suspended* (p. 25). Use the counting to drown out other thoughts, counting faster if that helps. When you're ready, your counting will slow down on its own. As you become less distracted, nothing will be in your mind except for the numbers themselves. This state is the final preparation for *Empty Mind*.

Step Five:

EMPTYING
THE MIND

AFTER all the previous and necessary steps, your body is going to be calm and meditative. From the *Counting,* your mind will start drifting off to a blank and empty place. This state of mind is actually what we're looking for.

Achieving this *Empty Mind,* therefore, signals that you have accomplished many correct kinds of physical and mental alignment. All the benefits we mentioned before will be realized—calming, physical healing, mental perspective, cultivation of *chi.* This builds toward the vitality and carefree joy usually only associated with being young. That, in short, is the goal of meditation: "eternal spring."

HOW TO DO IT

As you continue *Counting* from one-to-ten in the previous step, the numbers start to become insignificant and the mind drifts away so that it's no longer focused on anything. Thoughts will almost certainly return, especially in the beginning. But if they won't stay away, don't fight too hard to empty the mind. Instead just go back to the previous *Counting,* then slowly try to pull yourself back towards the *Empty Mind*. In this way the *Counting* step works hand-in-hand with the *Empty Mind*—if you're having trouble emptying the mind, just start the *Counting* again.

BENEFITS

If the mind is distracted, it will misdirect the *chi*. On the other hand, when the mind is empty the *chi* will be very strong and go unimpeded where the body needs healing and growth. This is exactly what we're trying to achieve.

COMMON PROBLEMS

Sometimes people wonder how you know when the mind is really empty. To answer this, try picturing a train station. The trains are thoughts, and the empty mind is the gap after a train leaves but before another one comes. Our goal is to prolong these gaps for minutes at a time. As you can see, it can take years of practice to develop 15-minute stretches of uninterrupted, thought-free sitting.

III.

POST-MEDITATION

Chapter Six

SELF-MASSAGE

YOU'RE A LITTLE DAZED after a good meditation, kind of like waking from a deep sleep. The face and body sometimes itch, the joints and the limbs can be a little numb, and you might be disoriented about where you are.

Now's the time to do some self-massage.

These exercises are considered integral to the meditation, not something extra. The self massage is designed to distribute and guide the *chi* that's charged up in the body—in Chinese this is called *do yun* (導引). If meditation can be compared to giving water to a plant, then self-massage is making sure that the water reaches the plant's many branches and leaves.

Self massage takes a short period of time, usually ten to fifteen minutes. You can work longer on parts of the body that feel weak from sitting.

The massage covers three areas of the body: the head, the torso, and the legs. It's good to massage through loose clothing for the torso and legs; this helps reduce friction.

When you massage, put your mind into the areas you are working on—you should feel the massage while you are doing it, whether it's your eyes, kidneys, or knees.

6.1 HEAD

6.1a Rub the Hands

Start the self-massage by rubbing the palms and back of hands back and forth together about ten times to warm them up.

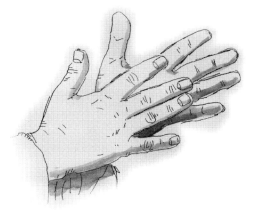

Fig. 6.1a Rub the Hands

6.1b Massage the Face

Fingers pointed-up (see fig. 6.1b), rub the face about three times, up and down.

Fig. 6.1b Massage the Face

6.1c Pressing the Eyes

Open up the hands with the fingers spread and pointing upward. Then with the thumbs pointing at your face, press the tips of thumbs into the eye sockets at the top of the nose. There's a cavity there. Press each thumb into that cavity as deep as possible.

Fig. 6.1c Pressing the Eyes

Maintain constant pressure for about one minute, so your eyes feel uncomfortable but without pain. Pain can be an indication that you have a problem with your eyes (too much strain or poor circulation to the eyes, for instance), or simply that you're pressing too hard. When you are pressing the eye, you're clearing the meridian for your eyes and helping the overall circulation of the body's energy. This is an acupressure technique.

If your body is relaxed and energy is circulating, you should see a lot of bright lights merging into a donut shape. The donut indicates that your meditation is successful, that your body is calm and your *chi* is strong. This bright donut will slowly fade and change to a darker, purple color.

6.1d Rub the Hands (fig. 6.1a)
Warm the palms again, to get more *chi* to your hands.

6.1e Massage the Face (fig.6.1b)
Rub the face again, this time spending a moment to rub your eyes slightly with your fingers.

6.1f Massage the Skull
Use the tips of the fingers to press hard on the skull, starting from your forehead and moving up and back over the skull. Try to press firmly with all fingers and move around so you cover the whole skull. Certain parts will feel like they need to be massaged—press deeper and longer in these areas.

Fig. 6.1f Massage the Skull

6.1ff Massage the Jade Pillow

After moving back and forth at least half a dozen times, start using your thumb to press into the Jade Pillow area, which is the base of the back of the skull—right in the center, in line with the spine, but above it. The Jade Pillow is the hard protrusion a few inches above the neck, in the back of the head. The Western anatomical term is "occipital protuberance." Push upward and into the indentation under the Jade Pillow area with the thumbs, for half a minute or so. (See figure 6.1ff.) Again, the massage should be uncomfortable but not painful. Like the eyes, the Jade Pillow is another *chi* junction with strong currents where several important meridians cross. Massaging here is very good for *chi* circulation.

Fig. 6.1ff Massage the Jade Pillow

6.1g Rub the Hands Again (fig. 6.1a)

Get more *chi* to your hands again, for further massage to the body.

6.1h Massage the Temples

Press hard and massage with the tips of the fingers into the temples (the flat area on either side of the forehead). Concentrate on any spots that feel like they want to be pressed.

Fig. 6.1h Massage the Temples

6.1i Massage the Ears

Squeeze the ears hard, grasping the ears between the thumbs and index fingers. Squeeze and pull at the same time, so you're always massaging— start from the top of the ear and work your way to the bottom. To finish, pull the earlobes downward. See figure 6.1i.

Fig. 6.1i Massage the Ears

6.2 TORSO

6.2a Rub the Hands (fig. 6.1a from the preceding head massage)
Again, you're getting *chi* to your hands in preparation for more massage.

6.2b Circular Massage of the Abdomen, Right
With the left hand over the right, press the heel of the right palm into your belly, following a circular line around the abdomen going down on the right and coming up on your left. Repeat this circular motion around the abdomen 36 times.

All these torso massages are traditionally done in multiples of 36, which has special significance in Taoist numerology. Also, it makes no difference whether you are right-handed or left-handed—the hand positions are the same for the torso massage. See figure 6.2b.

Fig. 6.2b Circular Massage of the Abdomen, Right.

6.2c Circular Massage of the Abdomen, Left
This is the same as the previous step, but with the right hand over the left and circling in the reverse direction (going down on the left, coming up on the right). Repeat 36 times.

6.2d Horizontal Massage of the Lower Abdomen
With the left hand over the right, press the heel and lower edge of the right palm into your belly and across, following a level horizontal line that crosses

the *tan tien* from one side to the other. Help move your hands by twisting the upper torso to the left and right. Repeat this left-and-right twisting 36 times.

6.2e Vertical Massage of the Front Torso

With the left hand over the right, press the heel of the right palm into your belly and press downward, following a line from the center of the chest to the *tan tien*. Come up using less force and repeat the up-and-down movements 36 times.

Fig. 6.2e Vertical Massage of the Front Torso

6.2f Rub the Hands Again (see figure 6.1a)

6.2g Massage the Kidneys

Lean forward slightly with the torso and reach behind your back. Massage the kidneys in a circular motion with the palms, coming up on the inside of the back ('inside' meaning closer to the spine) and pushing down on the outside ('outside' meaning farther away from the spine). Emphasize the heels of the palms when pushing down. Make sure that your palms are working on the soft area of the lower back, under the ribs and above the hips. The massaged area should feel warm. Again, repeat the circles 36 times.

Fig. 6.2g Massage the Kidneys

6.3 LEGS

6.3a Stretch the Legs

Straighten the legs in front of you, with the feet close together. Lean forward and try to hold the toes or ankles. Hold this for at least half a minute.

Fig. 6.3a Stretch the Legs

6.3b Outside Leg Massage

Open up the legs, to at least 90 degrees if possible—the wider the better. Lean forward and use the heels of the palms to massage the outsides of the legs from the thighs down to the ankles. Return hands back to the outside of the upper thigh, pressing in with your fingers. Push from the torso to move your hands. See figure 6.3b.

6.3c Inside Leg Massage

With the legs in the same position as in the previous step, use the same massage techniques but this time on the insides of the legs.

Fig. 6.3b Outside Leg Massage

6.3d Outside Knee Massage

For the last few steps you've been stretching your legs straight and flat on the floor. Now you can relax your legs by bringing your feet towards your body a little bit; the knees will come up slightly from the floor.

We're going to massage the soft depression around the bottom of each kneecap. Use the center of each palm to rub in a circular motion on these areas. The left palm should massage the outside of the left knee, and the right palm should massage the outside of the right knee.

6.3e Inside Knee Massage

Continue the same massage as on the outside of the knees, shifting the focus of the circular massage to the soft depression on the inside edge of each knee.

Fig. 6.3d Outside Knee Massage

Fig. 6.3e Inside Knee Massage

6.3f Final Leg Stretch

Straighten the legs in front of you again (repeating figure 6.3a), with the feet close together. Lean forward and try to hold the toes or ankles. Hold this for at least half a minute.

IV.
MORE ON
MEDITATION

Chapter Seven

OPTIONAL
TECHNIQUES

THE OPTIONAL TECHNIQUES are not offered as anything fancy; I say this because some instructional books have so many different techniques that you could never practice them all in fifty years! There comes a time when you have to stop learning new things and start practicing the ones you already know—that's why I want to keep the technique simple enough so that people will practice on a regular basis.

What's included in this section are a few straightforward variations that may help the beginner or, in a few instances, challenge the advanced student:

1. *Deep Breathing with Sound:* refinement for the student with some experience.
2. *Beginner Sitting Posture in a Chair:* for people who are unable to sit on the floor.
3. *Advanced Sitting Posture in Full Lotus:* for people with good flexibility, this is the optimum position.
4. *Crane Style Hand Position:* to help beginners with alignment problems.
5. *Buddha Style Hand Position:* a popular and easy way to position the hands.

7.1 DEEP BREATHING WITH SOUND

Deep breathing is one of the most important aspects of transforming *chi*. As I mentioned earlier (p. 28), the word "*chi*" also means "air" in Chinese; the air you breathe is called external *chi*. When you breathe deeply, the body helps transform the external *chi* (air) into internal *chi* (life force). Sometimes the extra technique of making sounds is used to accomplish this goal.

I usually teach two sounds: the first one is "oar" and the second one is a nasalized "hoi." Beginning students should try to practice the word "oar" for at least the first two weeks, and then the next two weeks work on the nasalized "hoi."

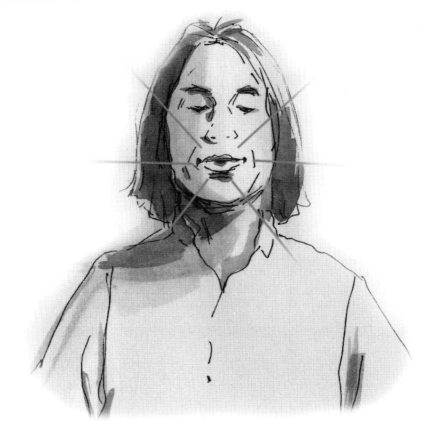

Fig. 7.1   Deep breathing with sound

During the five-step meditation, add an extra step after *Head Suspended* but before *Deep Breathing*. Take a minute or two to warm up with a couple of exhale-and-inhale sequences. Inhale deeply and then, bearing in mind the four breathing principles (long, deep, small, smooth), slowly utter the sound "oar" (or, later, "hoi") as you exhale with the mouth like a circle. Stay aware of the sound coming deep from below the navel, instead of a shallow sound from the throat or the chest. (Below the navel means the *tan tien*; deep-breathing is breathing from the *tan tien*.)

Try to exhale as long as possible without straining. After that, breathe in slowly, even though you may have to breathe in quickly because you're out of breath. This type of training can enhance the regular deep-breathing by helping you concentrate on each of the qualities—you can feel the sound vibrations for length, depth, smallness, and smoothness.

This deep breathing also helps strengthen the diaphragm, and even benefits the internal organs and nervous system. This makes sense because as some sounds can irritate people (fingernails scratching a blackboard), others can calm and heal the body.

So far we have been working on this long, deep, small, smooth breathing with sound. There's another technique I also teach, which exercises the diaphragm more forcefully. It's analogous to vigorously fanning a fire.

For this method, you use a short "Hing-Har" combination. Hing is for breathing in; Har is for breathing out. Repeat this combination rapidly, like short quick notes on an accordion. (Regular long, deep breathing is the opposite—like long, drawn-out notes on the accordion.) Hing is nasalized and helpful for pushing air down as low as it will go; Har helps shoot air out. This combination is not easy to do at first, but you should find that your *chi* will warm up much faster.

Of course, these sound techniques for breathing—either slow or fast—are not goals in and of themselves. You eventually want no sound. These sounds are only breathing techniques, not a mantra as in other meditative systems.

7.2 BEGINNER SITTING POSTURE IN A CHAIR

If you are especially stiff, you may want to just sit on the edge of a chair with both feet flat on the ground. The chair posture is also a useful way to make the best of a situation if you are on the subway or bus and you don't have a chance to sit in a lotus position. Sitting postures are independent of hand positions, and can be mixed and matched. (For an example of this posture with Crane Style hands, see figure 7.2.)

Fig. 7.2 Beginner Sitting Posture in a Chair

7.3 ADVANCED SITTING POSTURE IN FULL LOTUS

If you are comfortable with the Half Lotus, you should try the Full Lotus. This posture maintains the best alignment for the development of *chi*. It also prevents you from leaning too far forward and hurting your lower back. To get into Full Lotus, follow the instructions for the Half Lotus, then pull the bottom foot over the opposite knee so that legs cross with the soles of the feet facing upward. (For an example of this posture with Tai Chi Hands, see figure 7.3.)

Fig. 7.3 Full Lotus with Tai Chi Hands

7.4 CRANE STYLE HAND POSITIONS

CRANE STYLE A. *Elbows Out.* "Crane Style" means that the hands are touching the knees, pressing down on them. Here the hands are turned in, with the elbows out. This forces a stretching posture that creates more downward pressure on the knee. It's a good stretch for the ligaments. (For an example of these hands with Half Lotus, see figure 7.4.)

CRANE STYLE B. *Elbows Down.* As just explained, "Crane Style" means that the hands are touching the knees, pressing down on them. This time the hands face straight forward, with the elbows down. This posture is more relaxed than Style A (see figure 7.4) but lacks some of its stretching. (For an example of these hands with Sitting on a Chair, see figure 7.2.)

Fig. 7.4 Crane Style A with Elbows Out

7.5 BUDDHA STYLE HAND POSITION

As the name implies, this hand position is widely practiced in Buddhist meditation. It's higher-level than the Crane style, in my opinion, because more energy accumulates when the hands are touching like a closed circuit.

It's also easy to learn. Turn both palms facing up, with one hand laid on top of the other and the thumbs touching over the top palm. The hands sit in the lap. This posture is relaxed without as much stretching as the Crane Style (A & B), and it promotes roundness in the arms and upper-torso. (For an example of these hands with Half Lotus, see figure 7.5.)

Fig. 7.5 Half Lotus, hands placed in Buddha style

Chapter Eight

DAILY
PRACTICE

O VERVIEW. So far we've been learning the meditation exercises. But how can we get the full benefit of it all? The answer is consistent, daily practice. To really understand and appreciate the meditation, you have to do it on a regular basis.

Daily practice is a mental challenge. One of the problems is that meditation looks like you're doing nothing. This "do nothing" concept can be very difficult to understand at the beginning. At least with other exercises, you know you're doing something.

In weight lifting, for example, you can measure your biceps getting bigger. But in meditation, the yardstick is harder to see. So it's natural in the beginning to wonder if you're wasting your time.

Nevertheless, when you first try to learn any discipline you should have some faith in it. Give it a chance, and don't keep questioning. People under stress have the hardest time appreciating mediation at first. Try to be flexible, keep an open mind and see what happens. If you can get started, you can do it. All you need is to make it a daily routine.

HOW TO DO IT

You make appointments with people all the time. Even going to work can be a daily appointment. And you keep all those appointments. Sometimes it helps to think of your daily meditation as an appointment with yourself. In a lot of ways, it's the most important appointment of all — it makes everything else easier.

The best time to schedule your daily routine is right after you get up. Set an interval of time for practice, and whatever interval you determine, stick to it everyday. Consistency is very important.

A lot of people say they're too busy, that they don't have the time. My point of view is that there are 24 hours in a day, and you should take at least 15 minutes or half-an-hour for yourself. Even doing meditation half-an-hour, you're ahead because you have a clear mind, you need less sleep, and you make better decisions. In my life, it's just as important as eating and sleeping.

BENEFITS

Here I want to emphasize the benefits of daily practice. The best thing about having a daily routine is that you don't have to struggle each day to get started. It takes away the indecision, doubt and procrastination, so you can enjoy all the benefits of the actual meditation. The habit makes it easier to practice.

The daily practice also reinforces itself. Because you feel better — internally stronger, calmer, more relaxed — you develop a hunger for it, like a good meal. If you don't do it, your body will tell you to.

Daily practice is also like health insurance or medicine in the cabinet. If you get sick or injured, the meditation will help get your strength back even when no other exercises are possible.

COMMON PROBLEMS

The most common mistake is to tell yourself "today I don't do it, tomorrow I'll do it more." The answer is to do a little bit today, because if you leave it to tomorrow, then you'll never do it. That's why the best time to schedule the meditation is early in the morning, or any time you have to get up. You'll feel better the whole day if you do that. If you have a chance during the day, another few minutes are good, too.

Another common problem is setting the bar too high. You see that the meditation is good, but you're also daunted by the size of the project, so you make promises to yourself that are too hard to keep. Better to start modestly and try to build on that. Many times I've seen students who swear they're going to practice two hours every morning, but then they run out of steam and feel too discouraged to start again. In other words, it's a mistake to "force" meditation.

There's one more difficulty I want to single out: novelty. Meditation doesn't have much of it — it's short on new techniques, progress is subtle and, most of all, the practice is about realizing nothingness. The first day you do stretching and quiet sitting; ten years later, it's the same. Of course you're at a completely different level, but the pleasure in achieving that has almost nothing to do with the more immediate enjoyment of learning something new. Rather, the real sense of accomplishment stems from the calmness and the confidence that you have gained.

FIVE STEPS OVERVIEW CHART

STEPS	WHAT TO DO	HOW TO DO IT	BENEFITS	COMMON PROBLEMS
Head Suspended	Sit with your back straight.	Imagine your head and spine suspended like a string of beads.	Facilitates chi circulation throughout the body by decompressing spinal vertebra.	Backache; leg may become numb; mind may wander. Overcoming these difficulties is a necessary part of training.
Deep Breathing	Breathe from diaphragm. Each breath should be long, deep, small, and smooth.	When inhaling, push air down, expanding the lower abdomen. Reverse upon exhaling. Remain relaxed.	Most important nourishment (ahead of water and food); breathing transforms external *chi* to internal *chi*.	Can't breathe deeply enough; or trouble with long, small and smooth. Be patient; controlling breathing takes time.
Mind to the Tan Tien	Focus thoughts on *chi* reservoir, just below the navel.	Refer to pinky example; you can also touch *tan tien*.	Mental focus helps concentrate *chi* in its reservoir.	Locating *tan tien* and there; recognizing progress.
Counting	Count from 1 to 10 in your head, continually. Avoid counting breaths.	Ignoring all other steps concentrate on counting which should be separate from breathing.	Moves mind away from body; improves *chi* flow by removing mental distractions.	Count faster if you have trouble focussing.
Emptying the Mind	The abstract counting has crowded out other thoughts in preparation for this final step— No thought.	Let the mind go blank.	You're now peaceful and relaxed.	If mind still wanders, return to Counting.

DAILY PRACTICE CHECKLIST

WARM-UP STRETCHING

Stretching the Right Leg
Stretching the Left Leg

FIVE STEPS OF CHU MEDITATION

Head Suspended
Deep Breathing
Mind to the Tan Tien
Counting 1-10
Emptying the Mind

SELF-MASSAGE

HEAD

Face
Eyes
Face *(repeat)*
Skull
Temples
Ears

TORSO

Abdomen *(circular right, left)*
Lower Abdomen *(horizontal)*
Vertical Front
Kidneys

LEGS

Stretch *(straight)*
Leg *(outside, inside)*
Knees *(outside, inside)*
Final Stretch *(straight)*

Chapter Nine

Q & A

TECHNIQUE

1. There are a lot of instructions here—can I benefit just from sitting quietly? Isn't that what meditation means?

Sure, you get some rest and relaxation from sitting still, but why not get the maximum benefit for the time you spend? These techniques are easy to learn, though they require consistent practice. Also, physical alignment is important. If the body is not aligned correctly, you can injure yourself by putting stress on the wrong part of the body. (There's a Chinese expression, "dry sitting" (乾坐), for meditation that has a harmful physical effect and a wandering, daydreaming mind.) If you lean forward, for instance, it can press the backbone in the wrong direction. This will weaken your system, as opposed to charging it with chi. Even with a clear mind, it's possible to cause harm if you sit wrong.

2. I have no trouble sitting but my mind keeps wandering. Is this okay?

It's understandable that your mind will wander, but you should try to refocus as soon as it starts to wander. That's why we have five steps—if the mind wanders, bring it back to the step you're on. This is the mental training, and it's how you eventually develop the high-level ability to empty your mind. Part of the difficulty in teaching meditation is that the teacher can't reach out and correct mental alignment the way a physical posture can be adjusted. The teacher can't monitor your mind. It's different from tai chi, where I can move a student's hand if it's in the wrong place. The student has to do the mental part on his or her own. That's why the student needs a thorough understanding of the essence of meditation, and of the reasons for following certain steps.

3. Some meditation systems count breaths—Why count from 1-10 instead?
The counting is supposed to help you narrow your thoughts, one step closer to emptying your mind. However, if you count the breath, then your mind has to be aware of your breathing, but that just brings you back to the previous step, thinking about breathing! The actual numbers are immaterial; the point is to begin emptying your mind of meaning, so that nothing registers. In the beginning maybe you see numbers, but later the mind is simply empty. And if the mind starts to drift somewhere, draw it back with the counting.

4. Why long, deep, small, smooth?
Your lungs are like balloons. When you inflate a balloon, it's good to have a small amount of air going in smoothly so that the balloon will stretch slowly and evenly, without unnecessary stress. This is also the best way to strengthen your lungs and develop their full capacity.

5. If an Empty Mind is what we want, why do we bother with Head Suspended, Deep Breathing, Mind to the Tan Tien, and Counting?
Besides the physical benefits of each of the first three steps, all four together are necessary: they lead you to Empty Mind. You cannot skip the journey and go directly to the destination. Another way to think of the steps is in building construction—when the skyscraper is done, you take away the scaffolding. Each step leading up to Empty Mind is itself a form of meditation,

narrowing the thoughts and working on physical and mental alignment. When you have more training, the steps to Empty Mind will take a shorter amount of time. That is, you can achieve Empty Mind sooner. Even then, though, the sequence is still important, going through the same steps each time you meditate.

6. *Empty Mind depends on good posture—can you achieve Empty Mind while slouching?*
You might, but inevitably the body will disturb you. The principle of this meditation is to achieve and sustain a truly empty mind with the best body alignment. In practice, I don't believe you can achieve one without the other.

7. *I've heard of other kinds of meditation where you put the mind in the "third eye" instead of the* tan tien. *What's the difference?*
The third eye, located in the forehead area, is sometimes called the upper tan tien. It is possible to concentrate energy there, but I think it creates a problem gathering energy at the head instead of the lower abdomen. The reason is that *chi*—sometimes considered as a fire—should always warm from the bottom to be the most thorough and to build the biggest fire. If you have the fire on the top, the energy is probably uneven. This can be harmful. The body can become agitated and hyperactive. You feel aimless, like doing something but you don't know what; your energy is unfocused.

People also put the mind in different meridian points. In my opinion, this is inefficient. Putting your mind in the *tan tien* for a long time is more efficient and beneficial.

9. *I can't meditate for very long because my foot falls asleep, my back hurts, or my legs are in pain. What should I do?*
Meditation is partly a physical exercise. As with any exercise, it's important to recognize what's correct pain and what's not. If it's good pain, the answer is to tough it out or overcome it; that's how to improve. This is especially true with meditation because it's a healing exercise that will rejuvenate the body. But if the pain is incorrect, then you should stop before you injure yourself.

As I say in *The Book of Nei Kung*, "To the old phrase 'no pain, no gain,' I would add 'correct pain, much gain.' " If you practice the meditation consistently—always pushing a little but not too much—you should find that your body adapts quite quickly to the sitting position. If it takes longer to work through the blockages, that's usually a sign that there was some kind of pre-existing weakness or injury. Meditation will work through that—sometimes these problems can even be the effects of an earlier emotional trauma.

PHILOSOPHY

10. How can anything ever come of just sitting there, doing nothing?
In the *Tao Te Ching* (道德經), which is the most important book for Taoists, there is a central concept of *"wu wei"* that people have talked about for centuries, as in the expression 無為無有不為 *"wu wei wu yao but wei."* This roughly translates to "do nothing, yet nothing left undone." Meditation practice is a very good example of this contradiction—you try to be *"wu wei"* doing nothing, but after meditation, you can accomplish things easily. Things get done without any struggle because you are following the *tao*, the nature, of the world. A simple example would be to hold a stone up in the air. Let go and the stone will move by itself. The stone follows the *tao*, in this case the law of gravity. It has no difficulty going from one place to another.

11. Can you talk more about the mental insights that come from meditation?
When we meditate we try to achieve total emptiness to reach our unconscious or pre-natal state. That's where you discover your root, your own unique nature that makes you who you are. This personal nature, sometimes called *"sing"*, is a kind of mini-tao. Knowing your own unique *sing* is one of the most important benefits of meditation. If you don't know your own nature (*sing*, 性), you're going to be fighting the wrong battles all the time. Even if you win all these battles you'll still 'lose the war' because when you suppress your nature you will be miserable. You want to focus on living a long, healthy, and happy life. But once you recognize your *sing*, you can follow it. If you're argumentative, for instance, then maybe you're more suited to be a trial lawyer rather than a soldier; and if you're artistic, then maybe bookkeeping is not for you.

12. Taoism is supposed to be mystical, but you don't seem to talk about it.
The Taoism that we mention here is not the religious Taoism. It's the Taoism of the earliest time, which is a scientific, realistic, and imagination approach to life and to our problems on earth. This is where the yin-yang theories of creation, nature, medicine, and exercise come from. However, later on in history, some branches of Taoism became superstitious and more concerned with the supernatural.

EMPTY MIND
13. You say to empty your mind, but other kinds of meditation tell you to concentrate on something pleasant, like flowers or mountains or a tropical beach.
I think the answer to this question is an explanation of the value of an empty mind. I talked about this earlier ("Eternal Spring" in Chapter One; and in "Step Five: Emptying the Mind", of Chapter Five). The idea is that you rejuvenate the mind by giving it a rest, so that it can be sharp and clear, able to respond to all kinds of situations. Otherwise, your mind is clogged up with trivial matters that interfere with your thinking and health. Meditation, done correctly, provides even more recuperation for the mind than sleeping, when you have dreams.

When the mind is empty, your body benefits also because the *chi* will circulate better and in larger quantity. If the mind is thinking about something, it will affect the movement of the *chi* in your system. If the mind is at rest, it's empty and there's nothing forcing the *chi*. Then the *chi* will circulate in and around the body, and heal it. The *chi* will go where it's needed most. And that's what we want, that's the ideal situation. However, you will not get to this state for a long time.

Additionally, the process of emptying the mind is itself beneficial. The practice is a kind of concentration training that can be used for all the other areas of your life, whether it's reading, playing sports, painting, or thinking through your problems.

14. How do I know when I've achieved an empty mind?
When the mind is empty, your mind is at rest. But the world is still moving.

So look for signs that you have succeeded in turning off your senses by, for example, referring to a clock. You think you emptied your mind for five minutes but it turns out that it was twenty. Afterwards, your whole body is refreshed. You look like you had a good night's sleep. You're ready to do things—not hyperactive, but calm, relaxed, and seeking challenges. But to achieve twenty minutes of empty mind is not easy. I think it takes most people ten years of daily practice to be able to do that.

APPLICATIONS

15. It's nice to have this restful, empty mind while meditating, but how does it affect the rest of my life when I'm not sitting quietly?

The empty mind isn't just for its own sake. It's a training exercise that develops mental clarity, perception, and perspective. Meditation is a mind exercise—just like its physical counterpart, you look for strength and flexibility. Everyday we see examples of what happens when we lack for these mental qualities and lose perspective. People get into fights over a parking space and get killed. Something trivial escalates quickly into a life or death matter. It sounds so stupid, but it may happen to any one of us. We're all experts in other people's problems, but when it comes to ourselves, we don't do too much thinking or working for a goal that we know is good. The parking space is an extreme, tragic example of fighting over nothing, but we each need more personal perspective—we constantly have to remind ourselves what's truly important.

Meditation develops this perspective, the ability to put yourself in a situation and take yourself out at will. Taoists call it *chu si* (出世) (getting out) and *yup si* (入世) (going in). In other words, mental clarity is the reward for consistent practice.

INDEX

FOR MORE INFORMATION
ON OTHER BOOKS & VIDEOS
BY MASTER CHU,
VISIT
WWW.CHUTAICHI.COM